CORE SKILLS

SHARE IT:
USING DIGITAL TOOLS AND MEDIA

Miriam Coleman

PowerKiDS
press.

New York

Published in 2013 by The Rosen Publishing Group, Inc.
29 East 21st Street, New York, NY 10010

First Edition

Editor: Joanne Randolph
Book Design: Kate Laczynski
Layout Design: Holly Rankin

Photo Credits: Cover, p. 4 Jack Hollingsworth/Digital Vision/Thinkstock; p. 5 © iStockphoto.com/Christopher Futcher; p. 6 © David Kennedy/age fotostock; p. 10 Szasz-Fabian Ilka Erika/Shutterstock.com; p. 11 Mark Wilson/Getty Images; p. 12 Nicholas Prior/Taxi/Getty Images; p. 14 (bottom) Nicola Topping/Getty Images News/Getty Images; p. 14 (top) Fuse/Getty Images; p. 15 Ron Levine/The Image Bank/Getty Images; p. 16 Daniel Prudek/Shutterstock.com; p. 17 Dmitry Shironosov/Shutterstock.com; p. 18 Iakov Kalinin/Shutterstock.com; p. 19 Nice Monkey/Shutterstock.com; p. 20 Pixland/Thinkstock; p. 22 Alan Levenson/Stone/Getty Images; p. 23 Inti St. Clair/Blend Images/Getty Images; p. 25 © iStockphoto.com/Katherine Yeulet; p. 26 Cultura/Hybrid Images/StockImage/Getty Images; p. 27 John P. Kelly/The Image Bank/Getty Images; p. 29 John Nordell/Photolibrary/Getty Images; p. 30 © 2011 NBA Entertainment. Jesse D. Garrabant/NBAE/Getty Images.

Library of Congress Cataloging-in-Publication Data

Coleman, Miriam.
 Share it : using digital tools and media / by Miriam Coleman. — 1st ed.
     p. cm. — (Core skills)
 Includes index.
 ISBN 978-1-4488-7454-5 (library binding) — ISBN 978-1-4488-7526-9 (pbk.) —
 ISBN 978-1-4488-7601-3 (6-pack)
 1. Computer network resources—Juvenile literature. 2. Internet research—Juvenile literature. 3. Social media—Juvenile literature. 4. User-generated content—Juvenile literature. 5. Digital media—Juvenile literature. I. Title.
 ZA4150.C65 2013
 025.04—dc23
                                        2012007209

Manufactured in the United States of America

Contents

IT'S A DIGITAL WORLD

Digital **technology** is becoming a major part of everyday life. Each year, more and more people are learning to use computers and the Internet to do their jobs, express themselves, talk with friends and family, and meet new people.

Your home likely has a computer or a laptop, and your parents may have a tablet computer or smartphones. It really is a digital world!

Many schools have gone digital, too. Many classrooms have projectors so teachers can share information with their students.

Every day, people invent new tools to help people work and play together in the digital world. These digital tools can make it so much easier to find information and share it with your classmates and teachers. Digital tools can also offer fun and creative ways to present the information you learn.

WHAT ARE DIGITAL TOOLS?

Digital tools are electronic resources and programs that help you find and share information using your computer or other forms of technology. Digital tools can range from software programs and applications to devices such as e-book readers and cell phones.

SMART boards or whiteboards are like electronic blackboards. Many schools have these kinds of digital tools in their classrooms.

Online databases are another kind of digital tool. Your school library may have a subscription to one of these databases. They have collections of articles available for a student to read and share with classmates.

Digital tools can make doing your work much easier and faster because you can access millions of books' worth of information instantly. Digital tools also make it easy to share and talk with people across the world as though they were sitting in the same room.

Going to the library and checking out books is a great way to find information, but it can take a lot of time. Those piles of books take up a lot of space, too.

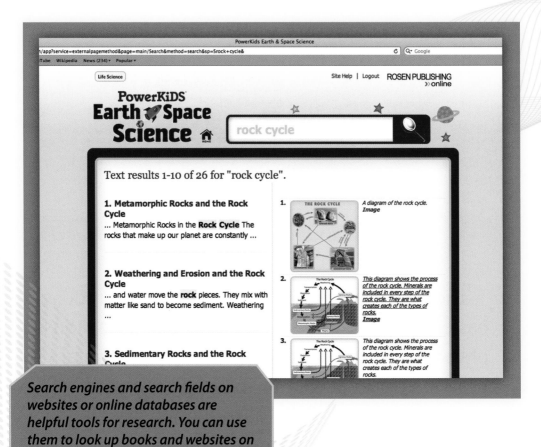

Search engines and search fields on websites or online databases are helpful tools for research. You can use them to look up books and websites on a topic, such as the rock cycle.

cience.com/article/222?search=prarie dogs

Earth & Space Science

Site Help | Logout   ROSEN PUBLISHING
» online

PowerKiDS
Life
Science 🏠

Print   Email   Cite this Article

Sections

Meet the Prairie Dog
Lots of Prairie Dogs
A Prairie Dog Day
A Planned Community
In the Nursery
One Big, Happy Family
Prairie Dog Towns
Empty Burrows, New Homes
Protecting Prairie Dogs
Find Out More
Glossary

Prairie Dogs

Next Section »

🔊 Listen

Meet the Prairie Dog

Have you ever heard of a **prairie** dog? Its name might make you think it is a dog that lives on the prairie. This is partly true. It does live on the prairie, but it is not a dog. It is part of the squirrel family. It is called a prairie dog because it makes a

▶ ⏹ 00:00   00:00 ✖ ◀━━
*Prairie **dogs** will bark to let others know that enemies are near.*
© www.istockphoto.com/David Parsons

Some websites may have videos or sound recordings that will add depth to your research on a topic. You can share the links with your classmates, too.

Using digital tools for research can be much faster, and the information is all contained on digital files stored either on your computer or the Internet. Search engines allow you to type in keywords or subjects to find millions of pages of information from all over the Internet. You can

QUICK TIP
You can read articles from most major newspapers and magazines over the Internet and do searches for articles on your topic in some publications' archives.

also use search engines to look for images or information in books or newspapers.

Digital versions of books called e-books allow you to access the text within books instantly. You can also search the text for keywords or phrases.

This lets you find exactly the information that you need.

A digital database is a collection of information that has been put together in a way that makes research easy. Digital databases are often organized by subject. They may contain collections of articles, sets of **statistics**, or links to other sites where you can find more information.

Digital tools let you visit countless museums and historic sites without ever leaving your house. If you are researching dinosaurs, you can check out Chicago's Field Museum website to learn about its famous Tyrannosaurus rex skeleton, Sue.

WAYS TO SHARE INFO

One of the great things about using digital tools for projects is that you can share your work with your classmates or teachers as soon as you complete it. Instead of sending your work through the mail or waiting until you are all together in class, you can use digital tools to send your work instantly.

If you are doing a group project on the weather in a certain place, you could have one of the people in the group take a video of you giving a weather report like those you see on the news. You could then share the clip with your class through a video-sharing website or even via e-mail.

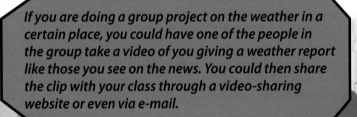

Send | **Chat** | **Attach** | **Address** | **Fonts** | **Colors** | **Save As Draft**

To: Caitlin Fraser

Cc:

Subject: My Research Paper on Tigers

Dear Ms. Fraser,

Attached please find my report on Bengal tigers.

Sincerely,

Jo Randolph

AA_BengalTi...ocx (58.9 KB)

In many classrooms today, teachers prefer papers to be e-mailed or dropped onto a file-sharing site, rather than receive printed papers.

E-mailing is one way you can share information. If you have an e-mail account, you can put the information in the body of the message. You can also send a **document** as an attachment to the e-mail. You can ask and answer questions over e-mail, and you can send one message to dozens or even hundreds of people at the same time.

Left: *Ask your teacher to show you some of the digital tools available on your classroom computer that make sharing information easier.* **Below:** *Video conferences are a way to share information digitally. Your school could become digital pen pals with a school in another country. You could work on a group project this way, too.*

Sending large files such as photos and videos as e-mail attachments can take a long time. Some e-mail programs will limit the size of the files you can send. File- and document-sharing sites such as Dropbox allow users to easily and quickly send large files back and forth.

Some of these programs will even **sync** documents across different computers. This means that if you make a change to a document you are working on at home, those changes will automatically appear in the copies of that document on your classmates' computers.

Your teacher might ask your class to create wikis about some of the world's tallest mountains, such as Mount Everest. A wiki is a shared online space where you and your group can work together to write an article.

You can share everything you learn with your classmates or even with the whole world by creating a website or a blog for your project. Websites allow you to present what you learn using media ranging from writing to photographs, art, videos, and **audio** files.

Your teacher may set up a classroom blog on which students can post essays or comment on topics being studied in class. This way of sharing builds an online classroom community.

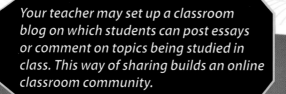

Your teacher could create a blog about other countries and then ask you and your classmates to add posts. If you are adding a paragraph about Rome's Coliseum, you could include a picture and then the facts you found out during your research.

You can organize information into different pages or chapters. You can even allow comments so that visitors to your website can share information as well.

The word "blog" is short for "web log." A blog is a type of website that uses a simple format, in which entries or articles can be easily added. These new entries will appear on the blog in **chronological** order, usually with the most recent entry appearing first. Blogs can also use photographs, videos, art, and audio files. If your project will consist mostly of writing, however, blogs are a good choice of format.

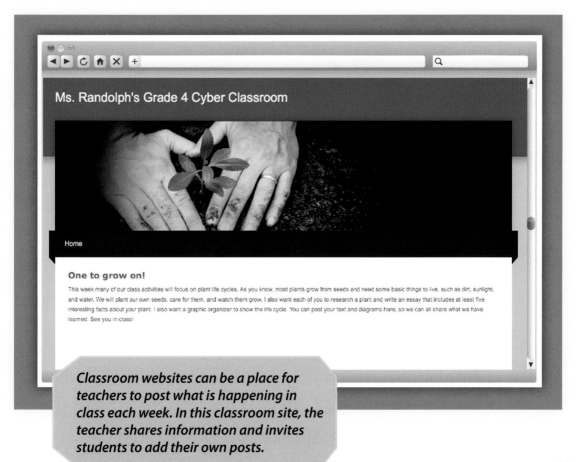

Classroom websites can be a place for teachers to post what is happening in class each week. In this classroom site, the teacher shares information and invites students to add their own posts.

Many schools have a computer lab where you can work on school projects and learn how to use digital tools to research and share information.

You can find a variety of free tools and programs to help you build a website, such as Google Sites or Weebly. Some of these tools will give you **templates**. All you have to do is fill in the information and graphics you want to use.

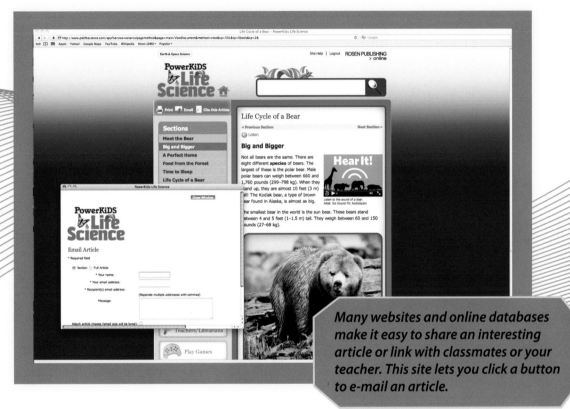

Many websites and online databases make it easy to share an interesting article or link with classmates or your teacher. This site lets you click a button to e-mail an article.

There are many digital tools out there that allow people to **collaborate** on projects, even if they are in different rooms or different countries. Programs like Google Docs allow multiple people to work on documents at the same time. The program will update the work as each person makes changes or adds information. It will also keep track of what contributions each person has made to the document.

Chat rooms and instant messaging services allow people to have written conversations in real time. This makes it easy to plan and discuss your work as you do it from different places.

This class takes part in the Global Schoolhouse Project, through which they can share information, ideas, videos, and more with classes in schools around the world.

If you are working on a group project, video conferencing applications let you get in touch with your partner to talk about your ideas.

Video conferencing programs such as Skype allow people to speak to each other or hold meetings in real time over the Internet. It is just like talking on the phone, except that you can see the other person and show him what you are working on.

USING BROWSER ADD-ONS FOR SHARING

A web browser is the software that allows you to access the Internet from a computer. It provides the frame through which you see the information and allows you to engage with it. Firefox, Google Chrome, Safari, and Internet Explorer are all examples of browsers.

Browser add-ons, such as Marker.to, let you highlight an interesting fact on a web article and send it to friends and classmates. They get e-mails with links to click on, which bring up the page with your highlights and notes.

Print   Email   Cite this Article

Sections

Wild Cats?

Lions

Tigers

Leopards

Cheetahs

Save the Wild Cats

Find Out More

Glossary

Investigate

» Bears

» Crocodiles and Alligators

» Sharks

Science Fair Projects and Experiments

Resources for

Wild Cats

Next Section »

Listen

Wild Cats?

When you hear "wild cats," do you think of kittens acting badly? Wild cats are what we call lions, **tigers**, leopards, cheetahs, and other members of the cat family that live in the wild.

All these animals share features with the

Tigers are the largest members of the cat family. They are endangered due to hunting and the destruction of their forest homes.
© www.istockphoto.com/Todd Burks

smaller cats we have as pets. They have ears that stand up. They walk on padded paws. They have claws that **retract**. They have strong jaws with sharp teeth. They are all meat-eaters. Let's learn about some wild cats with a "bad bite"!

Next Section »

Article Citation in MLA (Modern Language Association) format:
"Wild Cats." *PowerKids Life Science.* Rosen Publishing Group, Inc., 2012. Web. 2 Mar. 2012 <http://www.pklifescience.com/article/76/wild-cats>

Browser add-ons are programs that allow you to save, share, and comment on information you find on the web. Programs like ShareThis and Shareaholic add buttons to your toolbar that serve as shortcuts to bookmarking and sharing.

Your classroom computer may have browser add-ons that make sharing quick and easy. Check with your teacher to see what digital tools are available.

Smartphones have many apps, or applications, that let users share data. Always check with a parent or teacher before adding an application to a phone or tablet computer, though.

When you find a website you want to share, all you have to do is click the button and it sends a link to your friends or posts the link on social-networking sites, such as Facebook or Twitter. Programs such as Marker.to allow you to highlight and make notes on text that you find on websites and then share it with your friends or classmates.

INFOGRAPHICS AND OTHER WAYS TO SHARE DATA

Digital tools allow you to be creative in the ways you present information. Using **visual** tools such as maps, timelines, charts, and diagrams can be a very powerful way to share data in your projects. These tools are called infographics.

Most word processing programs have tools that let you create and insert charts, tables, and other infographics into a paper.

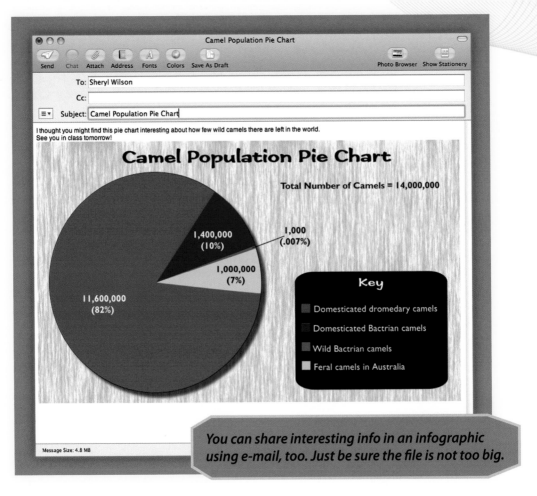

Send   Chat   Attach   Address   Fonts   Colors   Save As Draft   Photo Browser   Show Stationery

To: Sheryl Wilson

Cc:

Subject: Camel Population Pie Chart

I thought you might find this pie chart interesting about how few wild camels there are left in the world.
See you in class tomorrow!

Camel Population Pie Chart

Total Number of Camels = 14,000,000

1,400,000
(10%)

1,000
(.007%)

1,000,000
(7%)

11,600,000
(82%)

Key

◻ Domesticated dromedary camels

◻ Domesticated Bactrian camels

◻ Wild Bactrian camels

◼ Feral camels in Australia

Message Size: 4.8 MB

You can share interesting info in an infographic using e-mail, too. Just be sure the file is not too big.

You can use infographics to help tell stories in pictures. You can also use infographics to compare sets of information or to help your reader make sense of statistics.

Once you have researched and found the information you need, you can find many free tools on the Internet to help you turn the data into infographics. Programs such as Hohli and Tableau can turn your data into different types of charts and graphs. Google Public Data helps you find public data and statistics and then lets you turn that data into different kinds of infographics.

SHARING HAS NEVER BEEN SO EASY!

Using digital tools can be lots of fun. You might already be using them to chat with friends. Digital tools can also help you find facts fast and work together in cyberspace. Sharing information with classmates and friends, online or in person, helps everyone learn and builds a sense of community.

It is important to be responsible with digital tools. Only share materials that are reliable and will add value to your classroom learning experience. Have fun sharing information and listening to how people respond. Sharing has never been so easy!

As digital tools become more common in homes and schools, there will be new ways to share information. It has never been so easy to share information!

archives (AR-kyvz) Places where records or documents are kept.

audio (AW-dee-oh) Sound, especially when recorded.

chronological (kroh-nuh-LAH-jih-kul) Based on time order.

collaborate (kuh-LA-buh-rayt) To work together.

document (DOK-yoo-ment) A written or printed statement that gives information about something.

statistics (stuh-TIS-tiks) Facts in the form of numbers.

sync (SINGK) To cause to display the same information or operate at the same time.

technology (tek-NAH-luh-jee) Advanced tools that help people do and make things.

templates (TEM-pluts) Formats into which information can be filled so that documents or files do not need to be created from scratch.

visual (VIH-zhuh-wul) A piece of illustrative material, such as a photo, graph, or diagram.

Index

Websites

Due to the changing nature of Internet links, PowerKids Press has developed an online list of websites related to the subject of this book. This site is updated regularly. Please use this link to access the list:
www.powerkidslinks.com/cs/share/